TENDER IS THE BODY

ALSO BY ALISE VERSELLA

A Psalm for the Weary

When Wolves Become Birds

A Few Wild Stanzas

Onion Heart: Peel Back Your Layers

Five Foot Voice

Tender is the Body

Alise Versella

QUERENCIA

Querencia Press, LLC
Chicago Illinois

Contents

Tarantata

In a dream
Black as plague death
Like menstrual blood dried under my nails
After the night
Spent pleasuring myself

I dance.
The Tarantella: A thunderstorm of mandolins, guitars and tambourines

I lunge sideways
Slammed into the edges of a crowd
Pinpricks
Bursting through my body
Green and tilting
I move erratically

A girl must find the right tempo
To negate the *tarantolo's*
Poison

My body. Hysterical paroxysm
Shuddering as if in fit
Something ungodly must've overcome it

In the 18th and 19th centuries
Sexual desire in a female
Meant she was hysterical—heightened excitability
In extremes: sent to asylum, forced hysterectomy
The term *hysteria* used until the 1950s

In the tiny town of Taranto
Destitute women were forced
To sweat out the spider's bite alone

After the plague
400 women danced themselves to death
A state of *Choreomania*
Women and their hysteria

Now the *Tarantella* is danced at weddings

Deemed unlucky to be danced alone
Yet I twirl and I twirl and I twirl
Pull up my skirts and slide off my straps

Call me hysterical
Call me restless, anything but repressed
My body, dreaming and full of glory
Yes, glory be its tainted blood, pouring every month

I abstain from nothing. Let every pleasure come to me
A life that gets me off
Let me never orgasm enough

A hysterical woman.
Always dancing.

An Orgasm Magnified

I am the wine drunk
Caffeine withdrawal

I like the hand up my skirt
The paw on your chest
The lip-lock grid-lock of our through way

I paint a masterpiece between sheets

The sugar I'm craving is like an animal in my throat
A body that is not mine
      Free of shame; the belly ripple sheathe of skin

Here now I simply breathe you in
I don't doubt that a woman is more powerful naked

Than zipped
Into clothes
      She tries so hard to make fit

That certain limbs fit together better
Than her own
This muscle and sinew I give to you

Fileted like a fish
          Here are my scales

This bULGing eye
I gasp out of water
I die by the riverside

The best parts of me are coming to you

Playing Cards

Poker chips lay splayed like my legs and the woven blanket you wrap us in
I've cashed out, I've folded
Like the way my limbs bend
Folded into you

A bed can become a foreign street
And lovers, dancers of a tango in that foreign country's heat
Connect the way a tongue licks across teeth
Understands the words unspoken

Speak of sex
Speak of erotic poetry
And nude photography
And the beautiful curves and crevices and marks
The scars
When I touch them you are braille
I want to know the secrets you've only ever told yourself

And I want to taste your salt
Decipher its layers
Roll my tongue around its coarseness
Then let it melt

The Steam from Underground Reminds Me of Sex

I rise like the early morning temperature. Stretch out my spine like a feline, a jaguar in the canopies. I reach out towards that muted light, soaked magenta blush by the curtains. I am flushed and bed head like too much wine after nine pm on a Tuesday. My pillows and sheets leave the warm imprint of the girl I was in my dreams. It takes a minute to come back down to earth.

The grass and the trees are enveloped by a haze of humidity. The birds don't sing as sweetly, they are tired on the electric lines—they are haggard by the flight. I feel the weight of the longest month on my chest like a lover in midafternoon; how we touch and sweat and try to forget that snow leaden branches will hang just as heavily as this heat.

I drive with my arm out the window. The sun turning the hair blonde, the sun burning the skin. The way salted caramel hits sunburned lips and the salt from the waves caught between my teeth, like your tongue between—

Me and the peach are soft in spots, we bruise just the same, but goddamn we hang ripe for the taking, ready for the baking, the leavening.

I am ready for the way this last bite of summer will corrupt me. Leave me darker and a little more unrestrained. How the scalding days make us all a little savage, a beast pulling at his leash. Ferocious.

I'm going to snap that leash in half. Run through the torrents of rain. Then stand there as the world rumbles around me.

Deliciously it drips rivulets down my arms, like the pads of your fingers. Alarming the nerves. They sing more syrupy than those birds.

Our bodies' together hum wildly, vibrate madly. Pulsate like a heart—the rhythm riotous in the blood.

I beseech myself, "love this overheating of cheeks, the flames across breast how it fans out like wings from shoulder blades. Heaven's rebel angel burning, burning like this earth."

Burning, burning in love.

Tender Is the Body

Intimacy is that look you receive when you undress each other for the first time
Say wonderment

How could a woman look so beautiful in this lamplight?

My body is a gift I did not know I had been handed until you touched me
The way lips and the fingertips
And the breath warm like a radiator is to winter in a Brooklyn sub-let
Touch me

Intimacy is the way touch can make the body's crevices known
Deep sea between the sunken parts of my hips, the spaces that parallel each rib
Chart these depths
Say bathymetry

Navigate the intimate parts of my brain:
That which sinks its nails into the meat
Says I know what you are made of, I am made the same

I wonder who has ever really known me

We reach for each other in dark corners
I yearn to explore shadow and tendon
How it connects and is capable of withstanding tension

I watch our legs like loose strings tie themselves together
In the mirrored black of the T.V screen
That the body can lie prone while these organs tremor
Like how gravity prevents the earth from spinning outwards
Say tether

Say intimacy is not just sex
It is the building of a nest

The way a hummingbird may place hers between thorns in a thicket
At rest her heart reaches 250 beats per minute
Could you imagine a heart like that, how it could love
How it could be a place you might call home

You
Hopeless romantic
See the joy in everything
And the excitement is infectious a disease you let lie
A tumor—watch it metastasize

How dearly you hold on to the lifeline provided
By external hands
Unable to hold your own cold limbs

Child, how desperately you yearn to share your love
Don't you know you are love?

Holy lamplight in a mason jar
On a summer night
Fire burning the undercarriage of a spinning out car
Hydroplaning on slicked black tar

You are everything you seek in perfect symmetry

Dark and light like two sides of this globe holding strong to gravity
Spinning
       Spinning
Under the burn of the sun

You come undone
Again and again
And the unraveling is spun like sugar on a stick
You lick and it settles like a cavity in the teeth

This addiction is not quite harmful, you may not always lose the molar
This sweetness still keeps you from the bitter coarseness of stung tongues
The roof of the mouth aflame
You can't quite regret wanting to taste
That which came piping from the oven before it had its chance to cool

So you burnt the hand and the salve is not yet prepared
But how glorious to burn before you are ready
To laugh as the pasta water foams over the stove
Like rabid dogs who one last time just want to be free of the leash

We
Hopeless romantics
Do not think
Our hearts do not have the time
Forever aware of our mortality
We love now and messily
Let ourselves die a little now before the real thing comes to take us
And we can no longer feel
The blaze that trails behind us
Growing like a fire in the pinelands
The route we take through this life
Can warm your dark forests or burn it down

Yes we know we can burn inside it too
But we can't let that knowledge dampen our heart
When we love you we learn ever more how to love ourselves.

The Procession of the Year

Moments.

Fat and heavy like certain raindrops. Light and forgiving. Or a sharp slap across the cheek.

A moment becomes storm and then flash flood

Brimming at the sewer seams and busting. Pouring onto the lawns, making pools of the grass

It comes fast.

Life

And then, "you are what the sky washed up"[1]

You wring out the year from your flannel and search for where to place your blame

Say you were the wild horse that could not be tamed by the starting shot

So when the gate snapped open you pushed forth with a yelp

You think about the 364 days to come

And the 206 bones in your body

"How easily everything can be broken. How strong some things must be to endure." [2]

The coming storm will feel like a swarm

A hive you did not invite, but still, here they are displaced and searching for a home

The swallows will come with their wings to smoke them out of their nesting place

You swallow things that are not honey

Sometimes you dine on little deaths in different seasons

Flavor each with clove and cardamom

Citrus or sage

You still hold out your tongue to the rain to find out how each month tastes

If it changes the dying's shape

I stomp, high-heeled through the puddles, leading time's procession

Will myself with a childlike urgency to embrace the soaking cloak of the rain, just to be held

To live through the year means to love the mud

"Let me be Noah. And if not, then the flood." [3]

Opulent Women, Praise Your Virtuosity

I yearn to let go. Feel loose in my muscles, skin not stretched so taut, jaw unclenched, and no knots in the stomach. No fear in my shoulders looking over and over in the dark, in the car park…I want to dance. Drunkenly, like the women in the movies and on T.V who seem unencumbered by the consequences awaiting a girl who leaves the confines of her body on the dance floor with strangers. Who bends into the limbs of one-night lovers and inhales the sunrise at 4 a.m.

A young girl learns the feeling of being held captive by her body and some of us never shed the beast of that feeling. Gargantuan and looming over us, like shadows we must always assume to belong to the worst of our nightmares.

I mean we learn our bodies are a commodity, and some bodies cost more than others. The lives women lead always cost. We pay with our flesh.

Our whole lives we see the selling of our sex marketed to the pleasure of men and never our own. Sexualized, the body can never just be a body. Nobody gets by without the commentary on its size and shape, its wrinkle and fold, the way it hangs heavy, draped over our hearts, our heaving lungs.

What of the body, beautiful and not ghastly, not taboo, not something to cover up or shame? I like the softness of my hips and belly, the divots in my thighs, my lemon breasts and garden of hair. My contracting muscles, the way they billow like sails at my shoulders. The constellation of my moles and acne scars, a meteor shower torn across a sky of beautifully hued skin.

To be fully free in my body would be to bind my toes to the sand of a nude beach without the fear of eyes ogling or hands assaulting, to feel the wind harden my nipples and take the sea into my crevices and coves.

It would mean to move my limbs freely through the world in foreign countries and not doubt the strength of my flesh. To trust these legs and their mountainous terrain, its stray hairs—barbed wires guarding the inner sanctum of me.

It would mean letting the world see me enjoying what I want.

To know want as a girl is to know disappointment. A woman, truly free in her body, free in the world around her, learns how to take what she wants and call it necessity.

It is not greed and it is never too much and never not for her.

The well of her wants will not be emptied; will never evaporate into something smaller—a lesser want.

She will allow herself to want always the bigger, bolder things and trust that she deserves to have them.

She will stretch out the length of her torso and grasp with holy hands every summer fruit that hangs gravid from the branch, the orchard of her overflowing, spilling like juices flooding the chin.

The Curve of the Hip Loved Candidly

How many naked photos of me
Taken lovingly
Exist in the ether between
The space where
Deleted photos go?

What if you kept them
The one where my ass looked good
In the shaded afternoon light

What if it helps you sleep at night
Then I will let you have that
That piece of me not violation but beacon
Lullaby in the night

I take a nightcap from the bottle of gin
And recall the eyes of ex-lovers and how
The light swam inside of them

Sometimes I catch my own eye in the sideview
Mirror
How the sun catches brown
And the black rim
The kaleidoscope layers of iris
Fragile like paper

How it all detonates in a blink
The dislodged eyelash a wish

I collect paper—
Ticket stubs and receipts
Proof of us in ink
Stamped dates

Everything I love, kindling
Can evaporate like ash in water's care

Does the image of me hover there
In memory
In cornea
The deepest recess in the cave of the brain

Take one rose quartz and slip it
Under the pillow
Lay it next to your ex-lover's hair
In the morning
Dip your toes in the black pool
You did not have cleaned before winter of this past year
Swim beneath the burning sugar of one too many creme bruleés
And taste the blood under your teeth
From your split cuticles
The bitter chipped pink paint
Crush the clippings of old photographs by pestle in mortar
Crush them like chicken bones to broth in soup
Drink of the past and watch it leave your body from your dancing pores as you
sweat
How else would you dispel of pain and perhaps regret?
Take the rock in your shoe and suck on it
Siphon out the mineral taste of it
Bury your acrylic nails in the soil under a full moon

Come high tide you may take to the sea
And the tide will teach you
To love the ocean of yourself
Before the wave catapults you to a ready shore
With open arms
To the warm sand
No a warm hand
No the sun as it wakes your drunk ass up
Naked next to some random man
But the sheets are cool linen across the angry red landscape of skin the razor
keeps burning
Because God forbid you have stubbly legs
There are no spells to teach you how to love again
There is just tequila nights
And lipstick
And maybe the afternoon turns into evening and you simply say thank you
Goodnight
And you think
Please kiss me
Please call me again this Saturday.

Step Lightly Through This Grove

I have forgotten how to trust someone with my tree
To allow a gardener access to my leaves
Afraid he'll end up pruning too much of me and leave my branches sparse

I have forgotten balance
Unlike Marie* on her tightrope
Satchels of peaches tied to her feet
Manacles at her wrist and still
She crossed the Niagara blind

Marie, I don't trust myself that much

I've built so many boundaries to keep the worms from my apples
I think I stifled my appetite for the fruit

My orchard has a compulsion disorder, nothing can be moved a mere fraction
out of place
But you have uprooted me
And I splutter like I fell from the tightrope into the water

The birds are all screeching, *She better not be falling in love.*

I thought I wanted solace
To grow like a wizened crone-oak alone in the forest
To hold the edges of the blue skies and garner adulation for it

But I really want to be
Electricity
That strikes the tree and turns the seas fuchsia
I want to be the fire that starts in the trunk
And the dance depicted in the flame
I want to find the burning immaculate

I will step onto the wire foot by foot
Oh Marie, let him make me a mantle of soot.

Your Fingertips on My Exposed Kneecap Is the Most Erotic Spot I Could Think Of In This Moment

A body part never displayed sexually
Becomes the part of me that sets every hair charged like a battery
It's my Achilles

It's the skinned knees that hurt the worst
They take the longest to scab over
The landscape like alien mars once the gravel and the blood fuse

I think you could smooth
The scarred skin, I'd even hand you the oil
Maybe the pores would yield to you, thirsty craters on a foreign moon

I think a warm hand on a stiff knee is the best kind of curing
It's a bold move
        Just low enough

I've spent a lot of time with dirty knees
Burying things
I am quite afraid to get up and clean them off
My advertisement
That though a joint bends doesn't always mean it should

I used to play stiff as a board
My knees tan first
The skin there thinner than
The thicker parts

I don't want to hold your hand
Take both knees
The knobs of me that walk away
Say something and I will stay

Say anything about this bone in its socket
The extension of the limb
Punk rock knees in ripped jeans
Stubble, in the sun

One day a wrinkle and
The newborn pink of a puckered-up wound.

Produce Aisle

My teeth ache
For all the cool juice of an overripe fruit
My lips and the trickle onto chin
Fingertips
Remember the stain
The flesh and pith under nails I lick clean

It's all wanting

To bite into something called sustenance and find pleasure
We ask of each other,
"Will you sustain me?"
Can anybody ever really do that for another?

At some point the fruit rots, mold furs over skin

I think my favorite part is where it all begins
That firm flesh consistently poked at
To see if it gives
Retracts at your touch
And then yields

The cleave of teeth through peel
I inspect the imprint of my teeth
How bright white in the apple's meat
How it holds my shape

You watch my face as I eat and there is something sexual in each swallow

There is always a taking
Something
Is not always exchanged

Sometimes I devour the core of the apple
Wonder about the seeds and god

We plant things between us
And hope for orchards
        That under our care they will bear produce

What else could we possibly produce,
What with our beating blood
And our entwined hands?

Celtic Knot Ceremony Pantoum

Consider the knots that nature forms in bark and those humans tie
Believing that they're in love, that their bonds are strong and unbreakable
When even the oak trunk can fracture: roots unbound from the ground, with
the strike of lightning
What made you think your ropes would hold me?

I believed I was in love, that our bonds were strong and unbreakable
But even children and their mothers come untethered; the doula severs the
umbilical cord
What made you think your ropes would hold me?
They say wherever a Navajo buries his umbilical cord is his home

But we have come untethered; the doula severed the umbilical cord
We are waterlogged in Lafayette Cemetery, displaced from the ground
You buried us somewhere I can no longer call home
Home is gone

A waterlogged cemetery, my body displaced from the ground
Remains of us floating like dead fish to the top, silver bellied

Home is gone
My wrists are scarred from breaking free of your ropes

All that remains, dead fish, silver bellied
You did not consider the knots
My wrists breaking free from your ropes
Your oak tree has fractured; she unbound her roots from the ground.

Didn't you see the lightning?

A Woman Learns Small Bites as Politeness

It is impolite to devour anything. Devour as in consume wholly—with pleasure.
God forbid a woman be seen shoveling sustenance into her mouth, no, instead
she slinks home to the corners of her pantry to do so in private. Pleasure is the
part men don't seem to want to let women have. As if it's something one can
hand out like a ration. Women are taught to ration. Too much is a bad thing
because there will never be enough. The truth in the matter is that there never
seems to be enough for *her*. Men get their fair share. Of success, of meat, of sex.
Women are always taught to share and serve everyone but themselves first.

I am told I eat too much.

Disordered eating prevails in 9% of the US population and I am convinced it
begins in the kitchen. When you are poor you fear the food will run out, so you
starve—just a bit. When you are no longer, you begin to fear the weight
collecting on your hips and so you starve—just a bit. And the world tells you
how pretty you look—so thin! And the malnourished get even thinner. Become
ghost.

I become ghost at my kitchen table. My father never looks up from his meal. Except to tell my mother she doesn't need seconds, or she used too much garlic. He never asks about my day, never says thank you for this meal.

A woman's work is thankless. No accolades for best supporting wife or leading parent. But one must be both.

I am neither and I am looked at as if there must be something wrong with me for not wanting it. For not wanting to share, serve myself last. For not depriving myself of all I wish to consume and consume without shame. Watch me lick my plate clean. How gruesome as I tongue my fingers for salt and sweet and savor everything I could access.

Consider yourself lucky that I permit you access to my widening hips and supple flesh, how consumption becomes a meditation on loving. Cellulite a map of where to place your fingertips. I want that butter dripping and I want that second scoop of pudding, pile my sandwich until it looks like the layers of the earth's core. I will ask for more and then I will ask for dessert.

I am not surviving in a desert I am flourishing in a utopia of meals lovingly prepared to nourish and soothe. I want a peach's soft flesh like your lips. I want the sweet tart bite of a strawberry like your teeth on my shoulder. I want the poultry's skin crisp with rosemary. I want the sour lemon rind and the bitter aperitif in a frosted glass, the ice cubes clinking to my delight.

Do not tell me the sight of my enjoyment is impolite. That a woman should ever take small bites of the world she is constantly served. That she should settle for the scraps or "God's leftovers". I will make a meal of the very table the men feast from, the rich men, stockpiling goods they were never taught to share, I stole them. I did not hide the stains from around the corners of my mouth. Witness my thievery.

I like watching Nigella Lawson, raven-haired, voluptuous beauty cook a meal and taste it. When she looks at the camera and says, "oh just a bit more."

I want to see women enjoying more. I want to see poor men, like my father once was, enjoying everything and basking in the joy being consumed around him.

"Just a bit more." Until there is no more. Until we are ghost and dust and the cutlery rusts in the dirty sink.

Acknowledgments

"Tarantata" previously published in *Ellipsis...Literature and Art* Volume 59 April 2023

"An Orgasm Magnified" previously published in *Steam Ticket* Volume 23 May 2020

"The Steam from Underground Reminds Me of Sex" previously published as "Burning in Love," *Elephant Journal*

"Tender is the Body" previously published in *COG Magazine* November 2019

"Love Harder, Love Still" previously published in *Firebrand Anthology* White Stag August 2021

"The Curve of the Hip Loved Candidly" previously published in *Seven Circle Press (CircleShow)* Summer/Fall 2020

"A Spell to Love Again" previously published in *Academy of the Heart and Mind* November 2020

"Celtic Knot Ceremony Pantoum" previously published in *The Loch Raven Review* November 2022

"Produce Aisle" previously published in *The Breakers Zine* Issue 17 2023

Notes

1. *Dilluvio* (*Hermosa*, Not A Cult, 2019 by Yesika Salgado)
2. *The Last Mastodon* (*The Last Mastodon*, Rattle, 2019 by Christina Olson)
3. *Antibody* (*Salt is for Curing*, Sator Press, 2015 Copyright © 2015 by Sophia Vatomsky)

*Maria Spelterini (sometimes spelled Spelterina and occasionally referred to as Marie, July 7, 1853- October 19, 1912) was an Italian tightrope walker who was the only woman to cross the Niagara Gorge on a tightrope on July 8th, 1876. She did it again July 12, 1876 this time wearing peach baskets tied to her feet. She crossed blindfolded on July 19th and on July 22nd she crossed with her ankles and wrists manacled.

CPSIA information can be obtained
at www.ICGtesting.com
Printed in the USA
BVHW022110300623
666648BV00004B/106